RUNES

RUNES

CATHERINE J. DUANE & ORLA DUANE

ELEMENT

Shaftesbury, Dorset • Rockport, Massachusetts • Melbourne, Victoria

© Element Books Limited 1997

First published in Great Britain by
ELEMENT BOOKS LIMITED
Shaftesbury, Dorset SP7 8BP

Published in the USA in 1997 by
ELEMENT BOOKS INC.
PO Box 830, Rockport, MA 01966

Published in Australia in 1997 by
ELEMENT BOOKS LIMITED
and distributed by Penguin Australia Ltd
487 Maroondah Highway, Ringwood, Victoria 3134

Designed and created by
THE BRIDGEWATER BOOK COMPANY

Printed and bound in Singapore

British Library Cataloguing in Publication data available

Library of Congress Cataloging in Publication data available

ISBN: 1 86204 133 4

ELEMENT BOOKS LIMITED
Editorial Director *Julia McCutchen*
Managing Editor *Caro Ness*
Project Editor *Allie West*
Production Director *Roger Lane*
Production *Sarah Golden*

THE BRIDGEWATER BOOK COMPANY
Art Director *Peter Bridgewater*
Designer *Stephen Minns*
Managing Editor *Anne Townley*
Project Editor *Caroline Earle*
Picture Research *Julia Hanson*

Computer illustrations *Ivan Hissey*
Endpapers *Sarah Young*

Picture Credits:
Bridgeman Art Library, London: Royal Library Copenhagen 19. C.M. Dixon:
front cover, (top, bottom left and right), 4, 5 (T), 7, 8, 10, 16, 20, 22, 23, 26,
32, 32-3, 40-1, 44, 46, 51, 53. Fine Art Photographic Library: 35, 38, 39. Werner
Forman Archive: Universitets Oldsaksamling, Oslo, front cover (bottom center),
27, Statens Historiska Museet, Stockholm 43, 52. Fortean Picture Library 21, 50.
The Hutchison Library: Sophie Molins 9. Zefa 34; Rossenbach 31; Maehl 49.

CONTENTS

INTRODUCTION

Runes are shrouded in the mists of antiquity. They go back beyond the oldest of religions. Similarities can be detected between ancient Stone Age carvings and Runic symbols originating from Scandinavia.

WHAT ARE RUNES?

F It is thought that the word "Runes" probably comes from the Gothic word *runa*, meaning "secret whisper." It is applied to a group of Nordic or Germanic-type alphabets that might have been developed initially for magical purposes.

Each Rune has a unique pattern and these patterns provide a means to unlock invisible realities that are considered mysterious and secret. The Runes, according to some scholars, are processes that carry

RUNIC INSCRIPTIONS WERE STYLIZED ACCORDING TO THE OBJECT THEY ADORNED.

and convey the fundamental powers of nature, and the use of Runes is intended to bring balance and harmony into life.

Each letter has a proper and significant name, forming an entire phonetic alphabet. The language represented by these phonetic symbols is the Old Norse language, that was common to the Scandinavian peoples during the first six or seven hundred years after the birth of Christ. The letters were modified in order to suit carving techniques.

THE CHRISTIANS TRIED TO SUPPRESS THE
RUNES, BELIEVING THEM TO BE ASSOCIATED WITH
MAGIC AND THE SUPERNATURAL.

DESTROY THE RUNES!

We don't know if the Christians of the 12th century were given to slogans, but if they were, this cry might well have echoed along many a famed Scandinavian fjord. We do know that Christians did try to suppress the Runes, which is strange, since they had accepted the Greek and Roman alphabets. What was so threatening about a Germanic alphabet?

However, the word Rune meant "whispered secret," and was associated with the communication of knowledge and wisdom as well as with the occult, magic, and divination. The study of Runes was driven underground, enhancing, if anything, their claim to secrets and hidden wisdom. But inscriptions, especially on stones and artifacts, have survived, largely unnoticed and certainly not easily deciphered, and this has been the key to their survival. The folklore surrounding the Runes – conferring them with hidden meanings, healing properties, and other powers – has appealed to many over the centuries. Today, Runes have a new and ever-growing following. They have escaped the label of being purely occultist and are now becoming recognized as an intriguing form of divination.

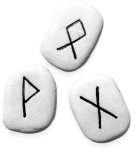

RUNIC SYMBOLS

THE MEANING OF THE WORD RUNE

As well as being associated with the Gothic word *runa*, the word Rune is also thought to derive from the German word *raunen*, that can mean "to cut or carve," and the Old Norse word *run*, meaning "secret." Cut or carved into stone, wood, and bone in ancient times, the Runes are mythically linked with the Norse god Odin, who is said to have gained the wisdom of the Runes by hanging on the Yggdrasill or "Tree of Life" for nine days and nights. According to the legend, 24 Runes – known as the Elder or Common Futhark – were revealed to Odin. Later, he wrote the *Poetic Edda* that consisted of 39 poems and songs, and became the proto-type from which the other Runic systems were devised.

They stayed me not with bread,
Nor with the drinking horn;
Downward I peered,
Caught up the Runes,
Screaming I caught them,
Fell back from there.

ODIN'S POETIC EDDA

F, U, TH, A, R, K are the phonetic characters featured in the early Runic writings of the oral songs and poems in the *Poetic Edda*. Today, most people who use the Runes work with a row of 24, that are divided into three groups or "families" of eight Runes, known as aettir. Each family of eight Runes can be linked to the eight directions on the horizon, to the seasonal festivals, and to various cycles of time and stars. They denote direction, place, and family, and the magical order of letters, or "staves," is fixed.

The 24 Germanic Runes are known as "Futhark," taken from the letter values of the first six Runes.

To inscribe an object with the
complete Futhark was a magical
act of great potency.

The Anglo-Saxons first gained knowledge of the Runes in Schleswig-Holstein and northwest Germany. Later, they developed 28 symbols that were then brought

RUNES OFTEN DECORATED MEMORIAL STONES,
AS IN THIS 11TH-CENTURY EXAMPLE FROM
UPPLAND, SWEDEN, C. 1020 C.E.

to England during the 5th or 6th centuries, and which continued to develop, reaching a total of 33 symbols by the beginning of the 9th century.

Another major form of the Runic alphabet existed in Scandinavia and Iceland. However, this alphabet had fewer Runes, 16 in all, which meant that one Rune served to represent more than one sound.

A majority of scholars stress the magical significance of Runes. The Runes were undoubtedly used in a special way for spells and magic, but they were also an all-purpose alphabet and were used increasingly for non-magical (i.e., gnomic, commemorative, or recording) purposes.

WHERE TO FIND RUNES

In Denmark, scholars have found 50 surviving Runic inscriptions dating from the 3rd to the 6th century C.E. Norwegian scholars have located some 60 inscriptions dating from the 5th to the 8th century, and there are approximately 50 Anglo-Saxon Runic inscriptions still in existence. These include such wonderful examples as the Runic scripts found on the Bewcastle, Leek, and Ruthwell crosses, and Franks' Casket. The right side of this casket is to be found in Florence while the rest is housed in the British Museum collection in London.

Sweden, not surprisingly, hosts the largest number of Runic inscriptions. Around 2,500 have been found so far, and most of these inscriptions are dated as originating from the 11th and 12th centuries.

FUNERARY ARTIFACTS WERE DECORATED WITH RUNES. THIS 6TH-CENTURY CREMATION URN IS FROM A LINCOLNSHIRE CEMETERY.

ORIGIN OF THE RUNES

Scholars have yet to agree on a generic source of the Runic alphabet. Some advocate that the Greek alphabet, c.600 B.C.E., is a prototype, while others have proposed that the Latin alphabet is the source, although neither claim has been proven.

Another theory suggests that the Runes may have originated in the ancient Etruscan culture of northern Italy. To support this theory, scholars point to the discovery of 26 bronze helmets, that were found in 1812 at Negau in the Austrian Empire. These helmets, dating from the 3rd century B.C.E., have a Germanic inscription engraved in the Etruscan script on them that includes the words "*Harigast I Teiva.*" Translated, these words are an invocation of the war-god Harigast.

RUNES MAY HAVE DEVELOPED FROM
STONE AGE ROCK CARVINGS.

Other scholars propose that the Runes developed from the Hallristningar rock carvings. The symbols were carved in the latter part of the Stone Age or early Bronze Age and have been discovered in parts of northern Italy, Austria, and southern Germany. These Runes, their pictorial symbols, and associated song names and lore, were the ancestral inheritance of the North Germanic peoples migrating south from Scandinavia.

One historical fact is certain, that the earliest inscriptions so far found were written from right to left, indicating an alphabet at least as old as the Hebrew language.

The shape of Runic letters, based on vertical and diagonal strokes and avoiding horizontals and curves, suggests that this was an alphabet designed for carving in wood.

EXPANSION OF RUNES THROUGH EUROPE

The current revival of interest in Runes reflects the fact that we are today searching for a deeper spiritual meaning to our lives, and seeking a more natural way of living through the ancient skills and wisdom of our ancestors.

The growth and influence of Runes were linked to the expansion of the Germanic tribes as the imperial power of the Roman Empire declined. By 410 C.E. the Visigoths (or West Goths, an ancient Teutonic people who began moving out of northern Europe), had sacked Rome and established their own empire. They invaded Spain, and occupied many parts of it right up until the Moorish conquest in the 8th century. Britain was also dominated by Germanic tribes – the Saxons, Jutes, and Angles – and by the end of the 6th century consisted of several kingdoms. The three largest were Northumbria, Mercia, and Wessex.

A GOLD BRACELET FROM A HOARD IN DENMARK. THE DESIGN IS BASED ON A ROMAN COIN.

HOW RUNES WERE CARRIED AND WHY

Runes were carried for many reasons. Purists saw the Runes as magical tools that could release the sources of energy that are within all of us, allowing us to realize our full potential. Others saw Runes in a more superstitious way, and treated them as lucky charms.

In Viking times, the warrior tradition was divided into three cults, each of which bore the name of an animal, such as the bear and wild boar. Among the most famous of these was the bear cult called Berserkers. These warriors are reputed to have had super-human strength because they drew on the Runes to possess the strength of the bear.

Spears were also engraved with Runes, giving them a magical title. The most famous ancient spear is the Rannja (the Assailer), that was found at a grave at Dahmsdorf, Brandenburg, Germany, and dates from c.250 C.E. Runes were subsequently carried on the rings and weapons of warriors to represent eternity.

Runes were also used extensively by a type of "shaman," who acted as a mediator, priest, healer, and seer. Runes were a part of everyday life, on both a spiritual and a magical level – both of which came into conflict with the Christian orthodoxy of the day.

The Viking Age lasted from 600 to 1000 B.C.E., and was marked by expansion and trade. Runes were widely used at this time and Runic lore proliferated.

When Christianity began to make pagan converts in the north, the use of Runes was threatened; they survived until the 12th century, when the Church decreed Runic use a danger and forbade its practice under threat of death. Despite these edicts and decrees the Runes continued to be used, and in the 20th century they experienced a renaissance, beginning with the teachings of Guido von List (see next section) in 1902.

Hitler allegedly used Runic symbols for political ends, causing an almost instant decline in their popularity. As a result of the Nazis' corruption of the Runes, the effect of this lasted for a number of years.

HITLER AND RUNES

 In his rise to power, Hitler adopted the Nordic myth of a super race. As he developed the Nazi ideology, he and some of his associates, such as Himmler, Goering, and Hess, drew on the work of Guido von List, who was born in 1848 and devoted his life to Runic occultism. In 1908 von List published *Das Geheimnis der Runen* (The Secret of the Runes), that comprised the theories of Armanism, which later became traditional in Germany. He also founded the Thule Society, a right-wing political club. Hitler later became a member and is said to have been influenced by Guido von List's teachings.

Von List died in 1919, but when the Nazis came to power in 1933, their basic dogma had its roots in von List's peculiar brand of occultism. The Nazis used von List's 18-Rune system, corrupting their original significance by introducing new symbolism that emphasized control and dominance. They appropriated the Sol or S-Rune as the insignia for the SS, the Tyr or T-Rune for the Hitler Youth, and the H-Rune or Hagal Rune for racial purity.

MYTHICAL CONNECTIONS

Runes are always coupled with various Viking deities, and Odin is considered the father of all the gods. A god of mystery, knowledge, disguise, and great power, he is associated with the elemental forces of war, death, wind, and storms. According to legend he could raise the dead, calm the seas, raise the winds, and extinguish fires using the Runes.

ODIN, THE FATHER
OF THE GODS,
COULD CALM THE SEA.

It was a mortal called Sig who inspired the legends of Odin. Said to have been king of the Aesir, a tribe who emigrated from the Caspian Sea region, he established a kingdom that incorporated the whole of Scandinavia. When he died, Sig was deified and renamed Odin – his burial mound is said to be at Upsalla in Sweden where a temple was dedicated to his memory. The wolf, the eagle, and the raven are creatures connected with Odin, and he is the giver of victory.

BRONZE STATUETTE
OF THOR, GOD OF
THUNDER.

HEIMDALL BLOWS HIS HORN TO SUMMON THE GODS TO THE LAST
GREAT BATTLE, THE END OF THE ANCIENT NORSE WORLD.

According to legend, Odin is not always to be trusted, and some of the myths show him giving victory to those who do not deserve it. Odin carries a spear, Gungnir, that has a three-bladed point and is designed to look like a raven. He is said to have had two sons, named Thor and Baldur. Thor is known as the Lord Protector of the Universe, and according to Viking legend, storms are the direct result of Thor charging through heaven in his mighty chariot.

The Th-Rune is the Runic symbol representative of Thor's hammer.

The Viking god Heimdall was called the Watcher of the Gods and known as the guardian of the bridge leading up to the heavens.

Njord is god of the sea, and the underworld guardian goddess is known as Mordgud.

Many of the Runes relate to a specific god; for instance, Thorn is associated with the god Thor, who in folklore is an aggressive personality. Other Runes relate to animals and nature, or to the signs of the zodiac and planets.

ODIN AND THE RUNES

Odin was god and inventor of the Runic alphabet, that he controlled and that was widely used in Scandinavia for magical purposes. When he hung on Yggdrasill for nine days and nights without food or drink, he had been wounded with a spear, meaning that he had been sacrificed to himself, in the same way that victims were sacrificed to him in real life, stabbed and hung on trees. In this way he penetrated to the world beyond death, and so gained mastery of the wisdom of the Runes and power over death itself. It was also believed that Odin could bring a corpse back to life by means of the cutting and painting of Runes.

FREY, GOD OF FERTILITY, HOLDING HIS SWORD.

The Viking god Frey was associated with the earth and its seasons, as well as fertility, and good fortune. Legend states that the god Frey is invoked for the sun and rain, and is considered to be the patron of festivals. The symbol for Frey is the ship called *Skiobladnir*.

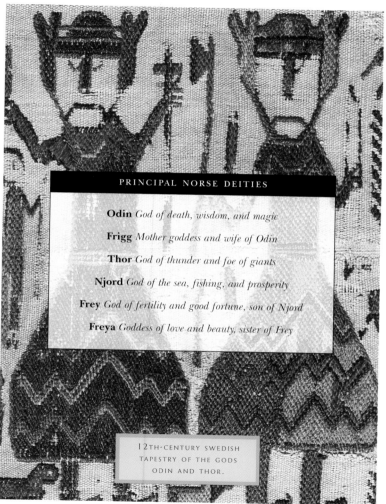

PRINCIPAL NORSE DEITIES

Odin *God of death, wisdom, and magic*

Frigg *Mother goddess and wife of Odin*

Thor *God of thunder and foe of giants*

Njord *God of the sea, fishing, and prosperity*

Frey *God of fertility and good fortune, son of Njord*

Freya *Goddess of love and beauty, sister of Frey*

12TH-CENTURY SWEDISH
TAPESTRY OF THE GODS
ODIN AND THOR.

THE MODERN RUNIC WORLD

With the continuing growth of materialism and technology, much of the modern world seeks to recover a sense of awe, mystery, and meaning. If you feel that you have lost your way in life, learning to make use of the Runes can be an invaluable aid. With the Runes as your guide, you will gain knowledge and, as a result, the spiritual tools to help you prosper on your chosen path.

Runes are not for fortune-telling as we have come to know it, but they can help us towards achieving wholeness. They can also act as messengers between our world and the gods, goddesses, ancestors, and non-human beings who can help us with the task of environmental regeneration to make our world a better place.

USE OF RUNES IN TODAY'S SOCIETY

- To restore the Odinic religion.
- As a form of magic.
- As a means of trading in fortune-telling.
- For commercial use – the selling of Runes in the form of lucky charms and jewelry.
- For use in the art of healing.
- As a means of self-development.
- Adoption by political groups.
- For use by scholars in the study of the Northern Tradition.
- For personal devotion.

MAKING YOUR OWN RUNES

Runes must be treated with respect as they embrace the potential powers of the universe. The motive of anyone working with Runes must be one of sincerity, love, and harmony. Most people who work with Runes will use the common Germanic Futhark symbols that are shown on pages 23 to 47.

There are many materials that you can use to make a set of Runes. Before beginning, it is advised that you have a safe place to store the Runes; they will take several days to make and must be left undisturbed.

It is important that you learn to master the symbols themselves. It must be understood that Runic writing has no power in itself. In the past, when sinister images were assigned to the Runes, it was done in order to instil fear and to manipulate others for selfish purposes.

A SET OF RUNE STONES
SHOWING THE
RUNIC SYMBOLS.

The Runes are given to us in love and are to be considered a blessing. Understanding and using Runes can enable us to further our own self-development and cultivate a more spiritual approach to the universe in which we live. By raising the level of our consciousness, we are able to adapt and grow, and to access more easily the potential inherent in life.

METHODS

Runes may be crafted from stone or wood. It is important to gather your own materials in order to establish your individual link with the Runes.

⊚ *If you are going to use stone you will need 25 flat stones, as similar in weight and size as possible.*

⊚ *The stones should be clean and may need to be washed to remove dirt, dust, and grime.*

⊚ *Each stone is then painted with a coat of varnish. When dry, paint one symbol of the Futhark alphabet on each stone. As you paint the various symbols on the individual stones, say the Rune name and visualize it in your mind. Be careful to copy the symbols exactly. The twenty-fifth Rune – Wyrd – will be blank.*

⊚ *If you are using wood, the best wood to use is birch or yew, these are traditional to Rune-craft. Use pieces of approximately equal length and size; twigs will work, or wood chips cut from a branch or small trunk.*

⊚ *Try to use paint made from a natural pigment. Viking legend relates that the symbols were stained with blood. Red paint can be used, as the color red has strong associations with the god Thor. Blue relates to the god Odin.*

⊚ *Runes may also be crafted from clay or from ceramic.*

⊚ *When the set of 25 Runes has been made, it is then necessary to consecrate them all.*

CONSECRATION OF THE RUNES

Consecration is a very ancient practice that is associated with most of the world's major religions. People, animals, and objects have all been the recipients of consecration at one time. It is a conscious act that implies a "setting apart," or being special in some way, and it incorporates a principle of cleansing. Runes are consecrated to indicate that they are unique, and this involves healing and cleansing. Consecration activates power within and without. The person who invokes the power of the Runes must do so for purposes that are good and noble and take the responsibility of doing so seriously.

Consecration takes place in four stages, as follows:

1. The first stage of consecration is called smudging, that means exposing the Runes to the smoke of smoldering herbs or incense. This stage is through the power of Air, representing the mind and then through Smoke, that represents the Spirit. Sandalwood incense is a good choice for the first stage.

2. Salt is used during the second stage of consecration and is symbolic of the Earth. The salt is sprinkled over the completed Runes.

3. Water is the third stage of consecration. Pour some spring water into a dish and fully immerse all the Runes.

4. The fourth stage of consecration is through Fire. Pass the stones through a burning candle.

When you have made and consecrated your own set of Runes, they are placed in a Rune-bag. This can be made from a plain piece of material such as linen or leather, and it should have a drawstring for closure. After this the Runes need to be activated.

The Runes are activated by holding the Rune stone, or wood, in the palm of the left hand. Making a cylinder with your right hand by slightly closing it, blow through this "cylinder" onto the Rune on your left palm. This routine is carried out for all 25 Runes. These Runes are now personal and should not be used by other people for any reason.

It will take time to get in touch with the energy of the Runes; the process involves meditation and visualization. Practicing these techniques for a period of time, you will begin to feel "at ease" with the Runes and gradually they become a part of your life.

CASTING THE RUNES

Runes were used to ward off enemies and diseases, or to promote good health or fertility, among other things. Today, they may be used to solve problems, or to help make a decision.

There are two principal methods of using or "casting" Rune stones.

1. They can be put into a bag and shaken, while you concentrate on the question or problem you need to have resolved. For this you will need to have a casting cloth – any white fabric which measures about 16 inches (40 cm) square.

Begin by tracing three circles on the cloth. A dinner plate can be used to draw the first outer circle, a small saucer will suffice for the second circle that must be drawn inside the larger one, and a glass or cup can be used for the inner circle. The inner circle represents the past, the second circle, the present, and the outer circle, the future.

There are many ways to lay Runes when you do a casting. One method is to throw out three Runes on to the cloth, noting where the Runes fall and the symbol on each of the Runes.

2. An easier method of casting Runes is to stand in a circle marked on the ground. Focus on the question or problem at hand, then gently throw the Rune stones, taking note of where they land. The closer they are to you, the more significant

RUNES CAN ACT AS
MESSENGERS WITH THE
ANCIENT WORLD.

For example:

◉ *If the Rune Kaunaz was cast and fell within the inner circle, it might mean that the person casting the Runes needs to express themselves more creatively.*

◉ *If the Rune Eihwaz has fallen into the outer circle, it may indicate that the person might need to work on a relationship.*

◉ *The third Rune may have been Laguz falling in the second circle, indicating that this person has many fears and doubts.*

◉ *Other methods of casting involve three sets of three Runes, five, seven, or twelve Runes.*

they are in answering your question. They would be interpreted according to where they fall in relation to the enquirer and to the other Rune stones, and also in their proximity to the circle, which is considered to be sacred.

For a beginner, it is best to remember that it is only through personal experience that you can come to discover the power of the Runes, and allow any feelings, impressions, or sensations to surface in a casting. This work is time-consuming and requires consistency and sincerity in desiring inner guidance and greater wisdom.

RUNES IN PRACTICE

Question 1

Is there a quick way in which the Runes can be used to help me cope with a relationship that is causing me concern right now?

The first thing you need to do is determine the problem. Then, by means of casting the Runes, focus on the issue that is causing most concern in the relationship.

Now choose four Runes at random. Four Runes are chosen because four is the number associated with balance and harmony.

For example:

- *The first Rune chosen could be Eihwaz, this indicates that perhaps assertiveness is a quality needed in the relationship.*
- *The second Rune could be Dagaz, indicating change, and may mean that one party has moved on.*
- *The third Rune, Uruz, would be suggestive of a new approach in the relationship.*
- *The fourth Rune chosen could be Isa, and this indicates a need to make things clear in order to strengthen the relationship.*

Question 2

Can Runes be used to conquer fears? I lack self-confidence.

John is worried about accepting a new job and has doubts about his ability. He has just recovered from an accident, so the issue here is John's hesitancy. He drew four Runes: Kaunaz, Laguz, Sowulo, and Raido.

For example:

- *Sowulo is associated with vitality.*
- *Laguz was suggestive of the fact that the fears are emotional.*
- *Kaunaz is the Rune of inner light, indicating that John has the power within to overcome his fears.*
- *Raido is the Rune that enables him to succeed.*

THE SYMBOLS
AND THEIR MEANINGS

In addition to understanding the mythical context of Runes, it is important to study their meanings on the material and spiritual levels. The most important source of information on Runic symbolism is the Anglo-Saxon Rune Poem, with each of the 24 verses relating to a particular Rune. Translated by monks from Old English into Latin between the 8th and 11th centuries, the poem didn't become available until the 18th century. It is believed that some of the pagan or pre-Christian content was altered to reflect later ideology, but despite this, the poem does reflect the spiritual code of the people of Northern Europe.

THE THREE FAMILIES OF RUNES

⊚ The first eight Runes form the Frey's aettir group or family.

⊚ The second group of eight Runes, or second aettir, is called Haegl's Aett. Just as the eight Runes in the first aettir were related to the god Frey, the second group of eight Runes is associated with the god Haegl or Heimdall, the watcher-god.

⊚ The final group of eight Runes is called Tyr's Aett.

THE RUNIC ALPHABET

FEHU
Frey

URUZ
Power

THURISAZ
Thor

ANSUZ
Odin

RAIDO
Wheel

KAUNAZ
Fire

GEBO
Gift

WUNJO
Joy

HAGALAZ
Air

NAUTHIZ
Necessity

ISA
Ice

JERA
Earth

EIHWAZ
Death

PERTHO
Hearth

ALGIZ
Protection

SOWULO
Sun

TEIWAZ
Victory

BERKANA
Birth

EHWAZ
Horse

MANNAZ
Man

LAGUZ
Water

INGUZ
Fertility

OTHILA
Ancestral

DAGAZ
Dawn

WYRD
Fate

1. FEHU/FEOH/THE F-RUNE

Wealth is a comfort to everyone,

yet each must give freely,

if he will glory in heaven.

This verse refers to the Rune Fehu/Feoh/the F-Rune.

The Fehu or Feoh Rune denotes the use and misuse of power. Fehu refers to cattle, and is a sign of wealth and prosperity. The Rune represents plenty, but also adds that wealth must be shared with others to win favor. Generosity is an important feature in many literatures.

THE FEH RUNE DESCRIBES WEALTH AS A COMFORT TO ALL HUMANS.

This is the first Rune of the Frey's Aett or group or family, and strongly connects to the god of fertility, known as Frey.

INTERPRETATION

This Rune can help in recognizing the true value of things. Possessions are not an end in themselves but a means to an end. While money can give access to power, the greatest (truest) power is the potential within us. This form of power cannot be bought, but must be developed and cherished.

The moon in Fehu suggests domestic security and wealth. It can also signify over-dependence on a mother. When Mercury is with Fehu they may bring about brilliant insight into financial matters, but when Mars is with Fehu there can be anger and forcefulness that may lead to frustration and to injury.

The number associated with Fehu is one that signifies unity. The color red, meaning magic power and strength, is also associated with the Rune Fehu.

The tree associated with this Rune is the elder, that represents endings and beginnings.

The planetary deity Odin, together with the goddess Frigg, rules over the Rune Fehu.

ANCIENT NORDIC MUSICIANS USING RUNE STONES.

 ## 2. URUZ/UR/THE U-RUNE

The wild ox is fierce,

with horns above,

a bold fighter who

steps the moor,

almighty.

This second verse of the Rune poem refers to the Rune that is known as Uruz/Ur/the U-Rune.

It is the symbol of the wild ox or aurochs. According to Viking legend, these now extinct animals were of great strength, fast-moving, and could carry great loads.

INTERPRETATION

This Rune indicates power but there is also a danger in untamed power. As the strong beast cannot be pushed, care must be taken to use power and energy wisely. The Rune encourages us to face the obstacles and challenges in life without fear.

According to Nordic mythology Uruz represents the space that lies between Cosmic Ice and Cosmic Fire, and contains the power of essence.

The tree associated with Uruz is the silver birch, is symbolic of rebirth and new beginnings.

The planetary deity Urd rules over the Rune Uruz.

3. THURISAZ/THORN/ THE TH-RUNE

Thorn is very sharp to everyone,
bad to take hold of,
severe to those who
rest among them.

The third verse refers to the Rune associated with the god Thor and is named Thurisaz/ Thorn/the Th-Rune.

Thor in folklore was an aggressive person- ality and there are many stories of his battles with monsters. This Rune therefore relates to standing one's ground firmly and being assertive.

Thurisaz is said to be the symbol of the ice demon that fed on human flesh.

The people of antiquity had a fear of being frozen to death in the cold climate of the north and being attacked by wild animals and then consumed.

THE THURISAZ RUNE ·IS ASSOCIATED WITH MASCULINE ENERGY, AS EMBODIED IN THE GOD THOR.

INTERPRETATION

This Rune can help you to overcome fears. It can help one to break down barriers.

When the solar powers are with Thurisaz it indicates a defensive nature and also carries the feeling of masculine energy. Because the blackthorn is a dense bush and has many thorns, it is usually associated with the Rune Thurisaz.

4. ANSUZ/OS THE A-RUNE

Mouth is the origin
of speech,
the support of
wisdom,
and for everyone
a blessing and a
confidence.

The fourth verse of the poem refers to the Rune that is known as Ansuz/Os/the A-Rune.

Ansuz means god and connects with Odin and the ash tree, the wolf,

THOR AND THE GIANT HYMIR
FISHING FOR JORMUNGANDR THE SEA-SERPENT.

and the raven. The essentials of this Rune are related to communication, wisdom, and ideas.

INTERPRETATION

This Rune is considered one of luck and can be used as a general invocation of the beneficial powers of the earth. It can also be used in creative work. We are warned to be on our guard when we play with words, since they can cause harm.

Ansuz is connected to the god Odin and also the ash tree with its deep and strong roots. This Rune is a symbol of primal power.

5. RAIDO/RAD/ THE R-RUNE

Riding in the hall
is very pleasant,
it is more strenuous
sitting on a strong horse,
covering the mile paths.

The fifth Rune is entitled Raido/Rad/the R-Rune.

This Rune is said to relate to journeys inwardly and outwardly. The Rune is also used in invoking the spirits of the dead. It is a symbol of change in oneself.

INTERPRETATION

This Rune signifies travel, movement, new horizons, and changes in life. It can also mean a crisis, a challenge to the way things are. Results do not come without sacrifice.

Raido is representative of the bright power of the sun-wheel. The oak tree, strong and durable, is connected to the Rune Raido.

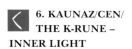 6. KAUNAZ/CEN/ THE K-RUNE – INNER LIGHT

Torch to all living
is pale and bright,
it burns most where
noble folk rest.

The sixth Rune is related to the word *kernan* in Old German and means "knowing." The Rune is named Kaunaz/Cen/ the K-Rune – Inner Light.

The god related to this Rune is Heimdall, the shining god. The Rune is connected to fire.

INTERPRETATION

This Rune suggests new energy and a positive outlook emanating from within.

The pine tree, that is long and slender, is associated with Kaunaz and helps one to value knowledge. The herb associated with Kaunaz is the cowslip, and this Rune is said to contain female energy.

A BRONZE VIKING WEATHER-VANE FROM
SÖDENALA CHURCH, SWEDEN.

7. GEBO/GYFU/
THE G-RUNE

Gift is for everyone
Glory and exaltation,
and for the needy
a help and sustenance.

The seventh Rune is named Gebo/Gyfu/the G-Rune.

The Gebo Rune is a reminder that there is a price to pay for wisdom and insight. It suggests the sharing of good fortune with those who are less fortunate.

INTERPRETATION

The Rune indicates compassion and generosity of spirit.

Gebo is associated with the color deep blue, and the herb connected to it is the heartsease. Gefn is the deity, and Gebo has the symbolic meaning of sacred mark. The ash or elm are the trees that are connected to this Rune.

8. WUNJO/WYN/ THE W-RUNE

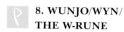

*Joy is needed not
by those that have
little want and sorrow
and have increase and bliss.*

The eighth Rune referred to here is named Wunjo/Wyn/the W-Rune.

This Rune is associated with Odin, who was also called Woden, in his role as the bearer of gifts and signifies contentment and joy. The symbolism of Wunjo is drawn from the weather-vanes used in Scandinavia.

INTERPRETATION

This Rune suggests comfort, good fortune, and happiness. It could signify a positive solution to any problems in either personal or business matters.

Symbolically, Wunjo means flag or weather-vane and is associated with the deities of Odin and Frigg. It represents the color yellow, the herb connected to it is flax, and the tree it represents is the ash.

WUNJO MEANS WEATHER-VANE
AND IS ASSOCIATED WITH ODIN,
ORIGINALLY A GOD OF WIND.

9. HAGALAZ/ HAEGEL/ THE H-RUNE

Hail is the whitest of grains,
it sweeps from the sky,
is whirled by the wind,
and turns to water.

A symbol of ice and hail, this Rune is named Hagalaz/ Haegel/the H-Rune, and is identified with the gods Urd and Heimdall. This Rune represents the potential within us.

INTERPRETATION

The Rune in this case helps to banish boredom and enables one to accept the challenges of difficult and frustrating situations.

The symbolic meaning of Hagalaz is the serpent, light blue is its color, and the ash and yew trees are associated with this Rune.

X 10. NAUTHIZ/NYD/ THE N-RUNE

Need is narrow in the breast,
but can often be a help,
if attended to early.

This verse refers to the Rune Nauthiz/Nyd/the N-Rune.

Nauthiz relates to need, necessity, and compulsion. The goddess associated with this Rune is Nott (goddess of night), who was the mother of Dag (god of day).

INTERPRETATION

The Rune represents great opportunities and success. With patient planning, problems can be overcome.

Nauthiz is associated with the deity Skuld, and has black as its color. The Rune is associated with the trees beech and rowan, and the herb snakeroot.

HAGALAZ IS ASSOCIATED
WITH THE SERPENT.

11. ISA/IS/THE E-RUNE

Ice is cold and slippery,
it glistens like glass,
is as bright as gems,
the field wrought with frost
is fair to the sight.

Symbolically this Rune resembles an icicle and is named Isa/Is/the E-Rune. The goddess connected with this Rune is Verdandi (one of the three Norns, or northern goddesses of fate). In the first line of the verse, ice is described as cold and slippery, like a floor made from glass, but it is nevertheless also beautiful.

INTERPRETATION

This Rune encourages meditation, and as a result answers to problems may surface. Isa is the Rune of self-containment and can help one to recognize the powers within.

Isa is associated with the god Verdandi and is symbolic of the icicle and the primal ice of Niflheim.

Like Nauthiz, the tenth verse, its associated color is black. The corresponding tree for this Rune is the alder, and the herb connected to this Rune is henbane.

12. JERA/GER/THE Y-RUNE

Year of fruitfulness,
is the hope of everyone,
when the gods allow the earth,
to give her bright increase
to rich and poor.

The name of this Rune is Jera/ Ger/ the Y-Rune, and it refers to the annual harvest period.

This Rune is a symbol of community and festival and is a representation of actions that are right and good. The god Frey is identified with Jera.

INTERPRETATION

The Jera Rune is a symbol of gradual improvement and is helpful during changes in our lives. It also enables us to be joyful, to celebrate life, and enter more deeply into harmony with nature.

Jera, whose color is light blue, is connected to the herb rosemary and the oak tree.

The god associated with this Rune is the fertility-god, Frey, and it is representative of both male and female energy. The Rune Jera corresponds with the earth.

THE JERA RUNE IS ASSOCIATED WITH
FRUITFULNESS AND THE HARVEST.

13. EIHWAZ/EOH/ THE EI-RUNE

THE RUNE POEM LIKENS THE PERTHO RUNE TO A GAME OF CHESS.

Yew is outwardly
a smooth tree,
Hard and fast in the earth,
the shepherd of fire,
twisted beneath with roots,
a pleasure on the land.

This verse refers to the thirteenth Rune named Eihwaz/Eoh/the Ei-Rune, that represents a powerful woman who is able to bring about good or evil. This Rune is also connected to death and for this reason can be frightening.

INTERPRETATION

This Rune teaches that there is nothing to fear. Death is another path on the journey of life. Transformation and development are inherent in life and offer limitless possibilities if we are willing to embrace the challenges on offer.

Eihwaz's symbolic meaning is the yew tree, a sign of protection and it is associated with Ullr. Its color is dark blue and is representative of male energy.

THE EIHWAZ RUNE TEACHES US NOT TO FEAR DEATH.

14. PERTHO/PEORTH/ THE P-RUNE

Chess is ever play and laughter
to the proud,
where the warriors sit
in the beer hall
cheerful together.

Of all the Runes this one is the most mysterious and is called Pertho/ Peorth/the P-Rune. The Rune is a symbol of the boundary between life and death. Pertho is the symbol of the goddess Frigg.

INTERPRETATION

This Rune is often seen as the Rune of fate and suggests a seeking of inner transformation. It is also related to song and dance.

Pertho corresponds to the aspen or beech trees and has as its symbolic meaning the womb, or a dice cup. The herb connected to it is aconite and the color is black.

15. ALGIZ/EOLH/ THE Z-RUNE

Sedge grows in the fern,
flourishing in water,
burning the blood of
everyone who touches it.

This Rune is used to ward off evil and is given the name of Algiz/ Eolh/the Z-Rune.

It is said to relate to the elk, to the yew tree, and to sedge. The god connected to this Rune is Heimdall.

INTERPRETATION

This Rune has uses in healing and protection, and can help to achieve a state of enlightenment.

Algiz corresponds to the color white and the yew tree. The herb connected to it is sedge, and this Rune has as its symbolic meaning the open hand, the flying swan, and the elk.

THE ELK, WITH ITS ENORMOUS
ANTLERS, RELATES TO THE
GOD HEIMDALL.

THE SUN'S ROLE AS A BEACON TO SEAFARERS
IS ASSOCIATED WITH SOWULO.

16. SOWULO/SIGEL/ THE S-RUNE

Sun to the seafarer
is always confidence,
When they move across
the fishers' bath,
'til the sea-horse
brings them to land.

This is the last Rune of the Haegl's Aett and refers to the sun as a guiding light to seafarers. It is named Sowulo/Sigel/the S-Rune.

The Rune is used as a symbol of salvation, light, and order against the forces of chaos and darkness. Sowulo is also representative of the god Baldur.

INTERPRETATION

This Rune helps us to contact our inner life force and indicates a need for a deeper spirituality. With the Sowulo Rune we reach the end of the second group of eight Runes.

Sowulo is associated with the color gold, the herb mistletoe, and the juniper tree. Baldur is the deity connected to this Rune, and it represents the male energy.

17. TEIWAZ/TYR/ THE T-RUNE

Tyr is a token
which has the confidence
of nobles,
It is ever moving
and in the darkness
of night never rests.

The Rune is called Teiwaz/Tyr/the T-Rune. Tyr the Norse god is concerned with law and order, war, and justice. This Rune represents a spearhead and is a symbol of divine justice, of strength, purpose of will, power, and of courage and determination.

INTERPRETATION

The Rune is used when courage and determination are needed and can help us take responsibility for our own actions.

Teiwaz is associated with the oak tree and represents bright red. Its symbolic meaning is the vault of the heavens over the cosmic pillar.

RUNES ARE CONNECTED
TO DEITIES AND TREES.

18. BERKANA/BEORC/ THE B-RUNE

Birch is fruitless
but bears twigs without
increase,
it is beautiful in its
branches,
is laden with leaves,
heavy in the air.

This secret Rune is sacred to the god Freya and is called Berkana/Beorc/ the B-Rune. It is a Rune of healing, of atonement for past deeds, and indicates regeneration. The Rune is also used in the aid of childbirth.

INTERPRETATION

This Rune is useful in relationships to restore a state of love and fruit-fulness. It is also used in times of new beginnings.

Berkana corresponds to the deity Holda and is connected to the birch tree. The corresponding color is dark green, and this Rune repre-sents female energy.

Regeneration and birth are asso-ciated with Berkana.

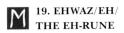

M 19. EHWAZ/EH/ THE EH-RUNE

Horse is the joy of nobles,
where heroes wealthy on
their horses exchange words,
to the restless it is a comfort.

In mythology, this is the Rune of the horses, that were regarded in many ancient cultures as sacred animals. It is named Ehwaz/Eh/the Eh-Rune.

The god associated with this Rune is Frey.

INTERPRETATION

This Rune is used when one needs help from the divine in times of trouble. It is also used for communication and helps restore a sense of control and balance.

Ehwaz is associated with the herb ragwort and with the oak and ash trees. This Rune is linked to the deity Frey and the corresponding color is white.

THE RUNE EHWAZ IS ASSOCIATED
WITH THE HORSE, A SACRED
CREATURE IN MANY CULTURES.

THE M-RUNE RELATES TO
RELATIONSHIPS AND KINSHIP.

 ## 20. MANNAZ/MAN/ THE M-RUNE

Folk in their happiness
are dear to their kindred,
yet all must depart
from each other,
because the Gods commit
the body to the earth.

This Rune is sometimes said to be the Rune of the god Heimdall, and is called Mannaz/Man/the M-Rune.

It relates to man as a species and is a Rune associated with relationships and kinship.

INTERPRETATION

This Rune holds the power to enable human beings to become integrated and to know themselves.

Mannaz, whose symbolic meaning is that of the marriage of heaven and earth, is linked to the deities of Heimdall, Odin, and Frigg. This Rune represents both male and female energy and is connected to the holly tree. The herb with which it corresponds is madder.

21. LAGUZ/LAGU/ THE L-RUNE

Water to land-folk,
seems tedious,
if they venture forth in
an unsteady boat,
the sea waves will foam
and the sea horse heeds
not the bridle.

Ancient tradition believed humanity originated from the sea. Water is a sacred and spiritual symbol and is associated with this Rune named Laguz/Lagu/the L-Rune. The Rune relates to the seal, the gull, and the willow tree, and has connections with the god Njord.

INTERPRETATION

This Rune indicates transition from one state to another. It helps us to integrate the ebb and flow of life.

Laguz, the sea wave, or waterfall, is linked to the osier tree. The associated herb is the leek. The corresponding color is deep green, and the connected deity is Njord, god of the sea. This Rune is representative of female energy.

RUNIC SYMBOLS OR DEITIES WERE CARVED ON CARTS AND BOATS FOR PROTECTION.

22. INGUZ/ING/ THE ING-RUNE

Ing was first seen among
the Eastern Danes,
departing over the waves,
his wagon ran behind,
thus the warriors named him.

Ing was one of the gods of fertility. The Saxon kings of northeast England claimed that they were descended from him. The Rune Inguz/Ing/the Ing-Rune is associated with this god.

INTERPRETATION

This Rune is concerned with male fertility and suggests new birth. Inguz also symbolizes a journey into the inner depths of the soul, where harmony and balance can be found to reside. Inguz could also signify the successful completion of a difficult task.

Inguz has associations with the apple tree, that is fragrant and graceful. The Rune is linked to Frey, god of fertility and natural fruitfulness, whose main attribute was his erect penis. It is represented by the male genital organs and may be the equivalent to the female Pertho.

THE RED BERRIES OF THE
HAWTHORN ARE LINKED
TO THE RUNE OTHILA.

INTERPRETATION

This Rune can be used to help develop latent talents, to guard family fortunes, and to achieve great success.

Othila, connected to the god Odin, has as its symbolic meaning land or property. The color associated with this Rune is deep yellow, and it is also linked to the hawthorn tree and clover.

 ## 24. DAGAZ/DAEG/ THE D-RUNE

Day is the gods' messenger,

the light of the gods

is happiness and consolation

to rich and poor.

The last verse of the poem refers to the Rune Dagaz/Daeg/the D-Rune. This Rune is connected to awakening the power that a new day brings. It is also concerned with the god and sage Heimdall.

23. OTHILA/ETHEL/ THE O-RUNE

Home is beloved of everyone,

if they can enjoy their

rights and labor,

and prosper in peace.

Concerned with matters of the home, this Rune is named Othila/Ethel/the O-Rune. The ancient peoples were more respectful of the wisdom of their ancestors than we are today. The Rune is used to invoke ancestral powers, and is associated with the god Odin.

INTERPRETATION

The Rune Dagaz is used to enable transformation to take place in life. It helps one to realize that light and darkness in life are opposite sides

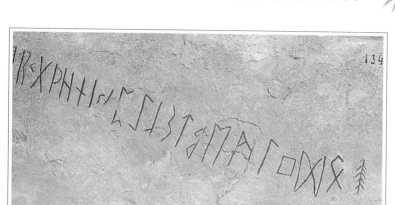

A RUNIC STONE FOUND IN SWEDEN
WITH THE OLDEST REPRESENTATION
OF THE 24-RUNE ALPHABET.

of one coin and that synthesis is possible. It also indicates the need for hard work.

Dagaz, which is linked to the deity Heimdall, is representative of male energy and is associated with the spruce tree.

 WYRD – THE BLANK RUNE

Wyrd, which means "to turn," is known as the Blank Rune and has no connections with gods, plants, or animals. This Rune is concerned with fate or destiny. It represents the unknown factor.

INTERPRETATION

This Rune is indicative of a major change in one's life and can even suggest death to a situation or event, or to a way of life.

Wyrd is the mother of the Norns, the primitive goddess of fate, and she governs the Web of Wyrd (pattern of cosmic destiny) between the root and the branch of Yggdrasill (the tree of life).

USES IN ANTIQUITY

In ancient times, people who worked with the Runes were put through long periods of training. The initiate was taught how to survive in hostile conditions and was given sophisticated physical, spiritual, and magical instruction. From the Viking legends we know of the Berserkers (see page 10) who went into battle fearlessly. But, it was not only the men who were trained in this way; Harald's army (700 C.E.) included women warriors called the Shield-Maidens, the most famous being Visma and Heid. Runes were inscribed on their swords and helmets for protection.

Hunting tools like knives and spears also had magical Runic names inscribed on them to signify their magical personality. It was believed that these charms or spells caused the enemy to go deaf, panic, or simply render their weapons ineffective.

In England, at Holborough in Kent, a 6th-century spearhead was discovered that had an engraving depicting the "Tyr" Rune (*see page 40*). Runic symbols were also carved on the stern of longboats as a means of protection and were known as "Brun" Runes to the Vikings. Runes for winning battles were called "Sig" Runes, and were found on weapons and the armor which was worn in battle.

PROTECTIVE RUNES
WERE OFTEN
INSCRIBED ON
VIKING LONGSHIPS.

Not only were Runes used for protection but they were also capable of righting wrongs; Runes for these purposes were called "Mal" or speech Runes. They were often carved or etched around areas used for courts and punishment.

Runes were chanted to aid conception, gestation, and the birth of a child. When the baby was born, Runes were cast to find the life path and name of the child. These were called "Biarg" Runes. At death the "Swart" Runes were used, and it was believed that these Runes helped the departed spirit to enter the world of the ancestors.

Viking legend also suggests there were Runes for mental agility called "Hug" Runes and Runes for attracting the love of a young woman. The tradition of using healing Runes continues today. "Lim" Runes were traditionally used for healing; today there are different Runes used to treat whichever part of the sufferer's body is affected.

"Fehu" and "Wunjo" are Runes connected to respiratory problems. "Thurisaz" is concerned with the heart while "Uruz," "Ansuz," and "Raido" are connected to problems with muscles, legs, and bodily strength. If one suffers from cysts, ulcers, abscesses, and fevers, "Kaunaz" is used. The "Gebo" Rune is used for toxic poisoning, and Runes such as "Hagalaz" might be suitable to encourage the healing of wounds, grazes, and cuts. "Isa" is for loss of sensation, "Jera" for digestive disorders, "Teiwaz" for rheumatism and arthritis, while the "Dagaz" Rune is for fear, distress, and mental illness. Runes form their own complementary discipline, and they are widely used today as an alternative or "complement" to more usual orthodox medicine.

HEALING WITH RUNES

There are several ways to heal with Runes. First, you should meditate with the Rune connected to the particular complaint. There must be silence and restfulness as you do so. Concentrate on slow breathing, closing the eyes, and focusing on the symbol of the Rune in question, and allow the Rune to bring up whatever images it calls to the mind. Allow the healing force of the Rune to bathe the person afflicted. The symbol of the Rune may also be worn in a piece of jewelry that the person carries with them permanently.

LINKS TO THE OGHAM SCRIPT

As well as boasting a Germanic origin, Runes are believed to be linked to the Ogham script, that is restricted to the Celtic population of the British Isles. The Ogham script is a form of archaic alphabet put to many and varied uses; it has been called "the secret language of the poets," and has formed an important part of the Bardic teachings in both Wales and Ireland.

Ogham takes its name from the Celtic god who was known as "Oghma," or "Ogmiua." Oghma was one of the masters of the poetic mysteries, and is clearly identified in Irish mythology as one of the Tuatha de Danaan, who were the original primal gods of Ireland.

In the southern counties of Ireland, 316 inscriptions in Ogham have been discovered, some of which refer to famous heroes, while others are believed to have been boundary markers. Fifty-five inscriptions in Ogham have been found in Northern Ireland, 40 in Wales, while one Ogham inscription has been discovered in Silchester, in the south of England. A few examples also exist in the Isle of Man and Scotland.

The Ogham script, just like the Runic Futhark script, was used for writing secret and sacred messages. Ogham formed a cryptic script and consisted of 20 letters linked to an element of nature. The alphabet was divided into four groups of five letters – the B, H, M, and A groups (the Futhark has eight groups of three, while multiples of three are also favored).

Some scholars suggest that each letter was linked to a tree, each tree being associated with mythological beliefs and tales. As can be seen in the Futhark script the letters were formed by straight or diagonal strokes.

AN OGHAM STONE. THE RUNES MAY BE ASSOCIATED WITH OGHAM SCRIPT.

OGHAM DIVINATION

Each of the letters is identified with a tree – i.e., Beithe "b" for birch, Luis, "l" for elm/rowan; Fearn "f" for alder – and twigs of wood from the various trees were inscribed with the appropriate letters and then thrown at random. The positions in which they fell and their relationship to one another was then read and interpreted. The throwing of sticks, called "Crannchur," is referred to in a medieval text called the Senchus Mor, in which it is said that when a decision or the answer to a question was required, three groups of wood were placed in a bag, shaken, and drawn forth again. According to the order in which they were drawn out, a decision or answer was provided.

Futhark features a 13th Rune, which is considered one of the most powerful Runes and represents a stave cut from a yew tree. This Rune is regarded as the stave of life and death. As in the Runic Futhark, Runes in the Ogham script took on magical and mysterious qualities and were used for writing spells and charms, for protection in battle and in life, for healing, birth and burial, and for divination.

LINKS TO ASTROLOGY AND NUMEROLOGY

As well as being connected to other early languages, Runes have links with astrological symbols and systems of numerology. Since antiquity, Runes have been used as a means of calendar notation that has evolved around cycles of time in relationship to the positions of the earth, sun, moon, and stars. Runic calendars were still in use in remote regions of Sweden up until the 19th century.

Ancient people had a sacred world view, practicing harmony with the natural environment. The earth and heavens were divided into four quarters, with Runes governing each quarter.

The ruling Rune for the east was called "Beorc," for the west "Ken," for the north "Jera," and the south was ruled by "Dag." The Rune "Gar" ruled the center. This basic fourfold division was usually further subdivided into quarters, half of which were halved again.

In the Viking age there were 24 divisions, each corresponding to one of the Runes of the Futhark. Multiples of three are generally favored in this system.

NUMEROLOGY AND RUNES

The 24 letters of the Runic alphabet not only represent sounds but numbers as well. Unlike modern numerology, using the Roman alphabet, that involves repeatedly adding the numbers to obtain a single digit (e.g., 645; 6+4+5=15; 1+5=6) and has only nine possible interpretations, Runic numerology has alternative systems. The most common has each letter of the Futhark representing a number from 1 to 24. Using this system the symbolic meanings are present.

HOW RUNES ARE LINKED TO ASTROLOGY

The Vikings believed the north pole to be the most sacred part of the sky. The "Nowl" star, that is now the present polar marker, is one of the "15 stars" that were used in ancient astronomy. All the 15 stars are ascribed qualities and exert certain influences. Close to Nowl are "Wodens" constellations, that are identical to the modern constellations of Ursa Major and Ursa Minor. Each of the 24 Futhark Runes has a ruling planetary deity.

SIGNIFICANT NUMBERS

Each Rune in the Futhark is assigned a number from one to 24. The number 20 marks the division of the circle in the Runic system. The day has 24 hours, the year has 12 months. The sum of all the numbers from one to 24 is 300 – this is significant because of the three. An important number in this system is nine. Odin is said to have hung on the yew for nine days and nine nights. There are nine circles that form a map of the Nine Worlds of Creation (on the Web of Wyrd, *see page 47*) delineated in Norse mythology.

- ⊚ *Sol rules Sowulo and Dagaz.*
- ⊚ *Mani rules over Laguz.*
- ⊚ *Odin rules Ansuz, Gebo, and Othila.*
- ⊚ *Odin, with Frigg, rules Wunjo, Mannaz, Fehu, Kaunaz, Jera, Pertho, and Berkana.*
- ⊚ *Tyr rules Teiwaz and Raido.*
- ⊚ *Thor rules Thurisaz and Algiz.*
- ⊚ *Loki rules Nauthiz and Isa.*
- ⊚ *Urd rules Uruz, Hagalaz, and Eihwaz.*
- ⊚ *Aegir rules Ehwaz and Inguz.*

NUMBER	SOUND	RUNE NAME	NUMERICAL MEANING
1 F	F	Fehu	*unity*
2 ᚢ	U	Uruz	*two horns, spiritual substance*
3 ᚦ	Th	Thurisaz	*triangle, enclosed energy*
4 ᚨ	A	Ansuz	*universal creation, the soul of the universe*
5 ᚱ	R	Raido	*universal life*
6 ᚲ	K	Kaunaz	*divine intelligence*
7 ᚷ	G	Gebo	*lucky seven, a gift*
8 ᚹ	W/V	Wunjo	*balance*
9 ᚺ	H	Hagalaz	*the nine worlds, substance of existence*
10 ᚾ	N	Nauthiz	*potential force*
11 ᛁ	I/Y	Isa	*static force*
12 ᛃ	J	Jera	*the 12 months of the year, harvest*
13 ᛇ	Z/Eo	Eihwaz	*unlucky 13, destruction/creation*
14 ᛈ	P	Pertho	*involution, entry of spirit into matter*
15 ᛉ	X	Algiz	*destiny*
16 ᛊ	S	Sowulo	*divine power*
17 ᛏ	T	Teiwaz	*wisdom, immortality*
18 ᛒ	B	Berkana	*twice nine, new beginnings, a higher plane*
19 ᛖ	E	Ehwaz	*the solar/ lunar number, transmission, correspondence*
20 ᛗ	M	Mannaz	*actualized force*
21 ᛚ	L	Laguz	*flow, facilitation of the will*
22 ᛜ	Ng	Inguz	*connection, expansion*
23 ᛟ	O	Othila	*the "weird" number, things outside conscious experience*
24 ᛞ	D	Dagaz	*day, 24 hours*

Mier þiðtrad **ASR** Fenris Ulfin: Tÿr miszer sÿna aðra Hönd: en þr Arisfera Ulfin til Ragna Röckurs: sofm XXXX Eddu Dæmisaga Utvÿsar.

TYR, THE NORSE GOD OF WAR, LOSING HIS HAND TO THE HOUND WOLF FENRIR.

FURTHER READING

ARCARTI, Kristyna, *Runes for Beginners*, (Headway Hodder & Stoughton, London, 1994)

BLUM, Ralph, *The Book of Runes*, (Oracle Books, Los Angeles, 1982)

COOPER, Jason, D., *Using the Runes*, (HarperCollins, London, 1987)

DICKENS, Bruce, *The Runic and Heroic Poems*, (Cambridge University Press, 1915)

EASON, Cassandra, *Rune Divination, for Today's Woman*, (Foulsham, Chippenham, Berkshire, 1994)

ELLIOTT, R.W.V., *Runes*, (Manchester University Press, 1965)

HOWARD, Michael, *The Magic of the Runes*, (Sam Weiser, New York, 1980)

MEADOWS, Kenneth, *Rune Power*, (Element, Shaftesbury, Dorset, 1996)

KING, Bernard, *The Elements of the Runes*, (Element, Shaftesbury, Dorset, 1993)

USEFUL ADDRESSES

THE CAULDRON
Caemorgan Cottage, Caemorgan Road, Cardigan, Dyfed, SA43 1QU, UK

FREYA ASWYNN
BM Aswynn, London, WC1N 3XX, UK

ODINIC RITE
BM Edda, London, WC1N 3XX, UK

ODINIST HOF
BCM Tercel, London, WC1N 3XX, UK

RUNE STAFF
142 Pheasant Rise, Bar Hill, Cambridge, UK

INDEX